COOKING SECRETS OF THE CIA

by

THE CULINARY INSTITUTE OF AMERICA

COOKING SECRETS OF THE CIA

by

THE CULINARY INSTITUTE OF AMERICA

Photography by Pavlina Eccless

CHRONICLE BOOKS

SAN FRANCISCO

Tim Ryan, Senior Vice President, CIA
Henry Woods, Project Manager
Editing by Jacqueline Killeen
Design by Sandra McHenry Design

Library of Congress Cataloging-in-Publication Data:

Culinary Institute of America.
    Cooking secrets of the CIA / the Culinary Institute of America : photography
    by Pavlina Eccless
        p.   cm.
    Includes index.
    ISBN 0-8118-1163-8
    1. Cookery.   I. Title.
    TX714.C8312   1995
    641.5—dc20   95-22251
                    CIP

Printed in Hong Kong.

Distributed in Canada by Raincoast Books,
8680 Cambie Street, Vancouver, B.C. V6P 6M9

10 9 8 7 6 5 4 3 2 1

Chronicle Books
275 Fifth Street
San Francisco, CA 94103

ACKNOWLEDGEMENTS

The Culinary Institute of America is a private, not-for-profit educational institution committed to providing the world's best professional culinary arts and science education. This book and the accompanying public television series enable us to reach millions of people who may never have the opportunity to take classes at our Hyde Park or Napa Valley campuses. We would like to express our deepest appreciation to those who have made this effort possible:

Cuisinart and their team of professionals for their vision in being the first company to step forward with support and their tremendous commitment to the project.

Freidr. Dick Corporation, which not only provides knives to our students, but also demonstrated their commitment to the school by becoming an underwriter.

The Danny Kaye Foundation and Dena Kaye for providing the ideal theatre in which to record the video series.

Our Producer, Marjorie Poore, for her creativity, drive, talent, and belief in the CIA, and to her partner and business manager, Alec Fatalevich, for his role in making the project a reality.

Project Manager Henry Woods, whose talents, organizational skills, and tireless efforts kept everything running smoothly.

The faculty and staff of the CIA, who shared their knowledge so openly and freely, and who worked so long and hard on this special project.

The tremendous staff of student volunteers, too numerous to mention, for prepping food, organizing *mise en place*, and washing countless pots and pans.

The book's skillful contributors: Joan Andrek for her holiday research, Ann Martin for preparing the recipes for publication, and Maria Renz for data entry.

The talented video production staff, who worked tirelessly both on and off location: D. J. Anderson, Wayne Moss, Michel Bisson, Skip Thela, Tina Cannizzaro, and Alice Galoob.

And finally, all the present and future students of the CIA—including our new home viewers and readers—who are our reason for being.

Tim Ryan, Senior Vice President
The Culinary Institute of America

The photographer wishes to thank the following stores for providing props: Crate & Barrel, Fillamento, The Gardener, Neiman-Marcus, Pierre Deux, Pottery Barn, and Williams-Sonoma.

CONTENTS

INTRODUCTION

Do you have a secret? Chances are you have several in your kitchen. After all, who doesn't keep at least a few closely guarded cooking secrets, either in the form of favorite recipes, special ingredients, or preparation methods? In some cases, a "family" recipe is so personal it probably couldn't be deciphered by anyone outside the fold.

Fine cuisine is often regarded as a secret, a pact made by the world's great chefs to develop palate-pleasing mysteries, never to be unraveled except by them. In fact, there could be a kind of "CIA" of great chefs, where their closely guarded cooking secrets are divulged only to those who can understand the formulas for extraordinary taste.

Fortunately, great cuisine has a CIA—The Culinary Institute of America in Hyde Park, New York—home to past and future great chefs and a mecca of teaching talent including numerous Certified Master Chefs (C.M.C.), Certified Master Pastry Chefs (C.M.P.C.), and even Registered Dieticians (M.S., R.D.). Best of all, there are no classified secrets at this CIA, but instead the understanding that the primary ingredient for consistently great food is simplicity. The Culinary Institute of America is pleased to unveil its award-winning formulas for good food through the Public Broadcasting Service cooking series *Cooking Secrets of the CIA*, to which this book is a companion.

Any great chef, particularly those who teach at the Institute, will testify that the greatest recipes are the simplest, those that make use of fresh seasonal ingredients at the peak of flavor and texture. The professional chef cooks simply, for it is in simplicity that appreciation for the balance and harmony of foods is developed. Whether the meal being created is a dinner for two or a feast for twenty, all good cooks start with the basics.

Most chefs agree that the fundamental lessons of ingredients, preparation, and timing were derived from their families. It is at family gatherings that most of us learn something about the kitchen, the foods we love, and the way these are prepared. It is at such gatherings too, that recipes are handed down and an irrevocable bond is formed, both with the food and the family that provides it. The combination of a special day, special company, and special foods can spawn a lifetime of culinary pursuits.

Holiday foods and the seasonal ingredients that go along with them are the basis for this book. Each recipe is a kind of celebration marking an event, a season, or a transition. Autumn, traditionally regarded as harvest time, is the starting point for this recipe compilation.

While many Americans celebrate Columbus Day, Italian and Spanish dishes are especially appropriate for a feast in recognition of Christopher Columbus. Our Italian Columbus Day Feast includes pesto, from Columbus's home city of Genoa, and dishes containing potatoes and beans, ingredients the explorer is credited with bringing back from the New World. Columbus's service to the Spanish crown is commemorated by a recipe for paella.

Autumn signals cooler temperatures and a corresponding need for more substantial foods. The appetizer and first courses in our "Starters" section make use of fall and winter foods such as wild mushrooms, squash, apples, and root vegetables. Halloween is celebrated with a frightfully good recipe—Pumpkin-Apple Bisque in Jack-o'-Lantern Bowls—that will delight both children and adults.

"The Main Event" section includes some complete menus and a selection of main courses for particular occasions, beginning with an autumn dinner. It is followed by two menus for that uniquely American holiday, Thanksgiving. A traditional

Thanksgiving Day menu is featured here, along with a contemporary menu.

The onset of winter means holidays with religious and cultural significance. We include two main dishes for Hanukkah, the Jewish celebration of deliverance: a contemporary entrée, and a traditional braised brisket to serve with latkes, a dish of great symbolism. (The "Starters" section includes another version of this dish, Cheese Latkes.) Christmas wouldn't be complete without a grand dinner such as the one we offer here. The winter holiday season is rounded out with two main dishes for Kwanzaa, an African-American family occasion that is now celebrated worldwide.

The Culinary Institute of America has long been a leader in developing delicious and nutritional recipes. There is probably no better time to introduce new light dishes than at the beginning of the New Year. Our luscious and light recipes are the perfect solution to holiday over-indulgence.

With the New Year comes a great American tradition, the Superbowl party. The secret to any party is good food, and these simple and zesty delights will make for a memorable halftime.

On the heels of the Superbowl comes

romance. We invite you to test the effectiveness of our Valentine's Day entrée, a task that we hope will prove enjoyable.

The Chinese New Year, based on the lunar cycle, falls between January 10 and February 19. Symbolic foods are served during this holiday to bring luck and good fortune in the new year. The Chinese consider the New Year their most important holiday, and every dish and ingredient is rich in tradition.

The cooking secrets of the CIA should prove to be no mystery at all. We hope you will use these simple, delicious, and festive recipes to begin some new traditions in your kitchen.

STARTERS

Our selection of first courses is drawn from a wide culinary world: a French-style terrine, Russian-influenced potato crêpes, a torte served with the smoked salmon and dill of Scandinavia, Jewish latkes, an Austrian savory strudel, crab cakes from the American South, and Italian focaccia. The soups are flavorful concoctions made from legumes, squash, and root vegetables, and may also be served as main courses for lunch or supper, along with a salad and good bread. The stocks are also invaluable as components in other dishes.

QUICK CHICKEN LIVER TERRINE

CHEF TIM RODGERS: This quick and easy terrine is one of my favorites, and will likely be one of yours too, since it is simple and fun to prepare. The ratio of butter to chicken liver makes it similar to foie gras in texture and taste. Chicken livers can be saved over a period of time in the freezer; when you have accumulated enough, treat yourself to this wonderful dish.

10 ounces chicken livers, approximately 1½ cups
1 cup (2 sticks) unsalted butter
1 shallot, minced
Salt, white pepper, ground cinnamon, and ground nutmeg to taste
¼ cup dry marsala wine
¼ cup heavy cream, whipped
Crackers or toast points for serving

Clean the chicken livers of any connective tissues. In a large sauté pan, melt butter over medium heat and cook the shallot until translucent, about 3 minutes. Add the livers and cook through, about 7 minutes. Add the salt, pepper, cinnamon, nutmeg, and wine.

Purée the mixture in a blender or food processor. Fold in the whipped cream and pour into a 6-cup terrine. Cover with plastic wrap and refrigerate overnight.

Serve with crackers or toast points.

SERVES 6

VARIATION: Substitute dry sherry or port for the marsala.

BRIE CHEESE TORTE WITH SMOKED SALMON AND DILL

CHEF TIM RODGERS: Kitchen tools need not be complicated; a piece of dental floss transforms an ordinary wheel of cheese into an eye-catching dish that can be tailored to any meal. Smoked salmon and dill are added to create an appetizer or an accompaniment for a dinner salad, while a quick substitution of fresh fruit preserves creates a dessert or breakfast dish.

1 wheel (about 2 pounds) Brie cheese
4 ounces thinly sliced smoked salmon
½ bunch fresh dill, chopped

With a nylon fishing line or unflavored dental floss, cut the wheel of Brie into three crosswise layers. On the bottom layer place a very thin layer of smoked salmon, then chopped dill. Place the second layer of cheese directly on the first and repeat the process. Finish with the top layer. Coat the entire outside of the torte with chopped dill.

Wrap in plastic wrap and place in the refrigerator overnight. To serve, cut the torte in half to show the layers and allow your guests to cut their own portions.

MAKES ABOUT 24 SERVINGS

CHEF'S TIP: Many substitutions can be made in layering ingredients, such as basil, preserves, pesto, chopped nuts, or ham.

CHEESE LATKES

CHEF MOREY KANNER: Latkes are a traditional dish for those of the Jewish faith. These fried cakes symbolize several things, especially the ancient Jewish liberation from Syria celebrated at Hanukkah. Although latkes are most often made with potato batter, Sephardic Jews use cheese, which is a tribute to a heroine of the liberation.

1 cup whole-milk cottage cheese
1 cup whole-milk ricotta cheese
3 eggs
¼ cup all-purpose flour
2 tablespoons sugar
1 teaspoon vanilla extract
¼ teaspoon ground cinnamon
Butter for frying
Sour cream for serving
Raspberry or lingonberry jam for serving

Combine the cottage cheese, ricotta cheese, eggs, flour, sugar, vanilla, and cinnamon in a blender or food processor and purée until smooth.

Heat a large cast-iron skillet over medium heat and melt butter. Spoon or pour into pan approximately 2 tablespoons of batter for each cake.

When bubbles begin to appear on the top of each latke and the bottom is golden brown, carefully turn to brown the other side. Drain on paper towels. Keep warm in a 200°F oven. Repeat until all the batter is used. Serve warm with sour cream and jam.

SERVES 8 TO 9

CHEF'S TIP: Cheese latkes are also wonderful for a brunch and as party hors d'oeuvre.

POTATO CRÊPES WITH SOUR CREAM AND CAVIAR

CHEF TIM RODGERS: One of my more delicious childhood memories is of fried potato cakes made from leftovers. This recipe is a refined version of that dish, and is easy to produce thanks to the food processor. I have used caviar to grace the crêpes, but chopped olives, thin strips of ham, or chopped fresh herbs are also appropriate garnishes.

5 tablespoons all-purpose flour
1 pound potatoes, peeled, cooked, and mashed (about 2 cups)
3 eggs
4 egg whites
¼ cup heavy cream
Salt and white pepper to taste
Pinch ground nutmeg
2 tablespoons canola oil or vegetable oil
Sour cream for garnish
1 ounce caviar for garnish

In a food processor, or using an electric mixer with paddle, blend the flour gradually into the potatoes. Mix in the eggs one at a time, then the whites. Add the cream to pancake batter consistency and season with the salt, pepper, and nutmeg.

Coat a large nonstick skillet or sauté pan lightly with some of the oil and place over medium heat. Pour in batter as for silver-dollar pancakes. Cook until golden brown, turning when bubbles appear on the surface. Cook until brown on the second side. Transfer to a 200°F oven and repeat until all the batter is used.

Serve warm, with a small dollop of sour cream and caviar.

MAKES 30 SMALL CRÊPES

VARIATIONS: Crème frâiche can be substituted for the sour cream; smoked salmon, country ham, or mushrooms can be substituted for the caviar.

FOREST-MUSHROOM STRUDEL

CHEF TIM RODGERS: This recipe emphasizes the versatility of its ingredients, beginning with the phyllo dough. Although it calls for goat cheese, you may also use cream cheese, ricotta, or even reduced heavy cream. This dish makes a great appetizer, but it can also serve as an entrée when paired with a salad or fresh vegetables.

2 tablespoons unsalted butter plus ¾ cups (1½ sticks)
   unsalted butter, melted
2 tablespoons minced shallots
1 clove garlic, minced
8 ounces assorted mushrooms (such as stemmed shiitake, cremini,
   button), coarsely chopped
3 tablespoons dry white wine
¼ cup crumbled goat cheese
1 teaspoon chopped fresh flat-leaf parsley
1 teaspoon chopped fresh chervil
1 teaspoon chopped fresh chives
3 sheets phyllo dough

In a medium sauté pan over medium heat, melt the 2 tablespoons butter and cook the shallots and garlic until translucent, about 3 minutes. Add the mushrooms and white wine and continue to cook 8 to 10 minutes until the mushrooms are cooked through. Remove from the heat and allow mixture to cool thoroughly. Preheat the oven to 400°F.

When the mixture is cool, add the goat cheese and fresh herbs and mix in well to form a paste.

Lay out 1 phyllo sheet and brush with some of the warm melted butter. Top with the second and third sheets, brushing each time with butter. Form the mushroom mixture into a cylinder at one end of the buttered sheets. Roll the mixture in the phyllo and brush the outside with butter.

Make small parallel cuts in the dough, about 1 inch apart and one third of the way through, to form diamond-shaped portions. Place on a baking sheet and bake until golden brown, about 15 to 20 minutes.

Allow to cool slightly and slice all the way through the cuts. Serve warm.

MAKES ABOUT 12 PORTIONS; SERVES 4 AS A FIRST COURSE; SERVES 8 TO 10 AS AN HORS D'OEUVRE.

CHEF'S TIP: An assortment of mushrooms will give this strudel varied textures and colors, but it is also delicious made with only button mushrooms.

CAJUN-STYLE CRAB CAKES WITH CREOLE HONEY-MUSTARD SAUCE

CHEF TIM RODGERS: Crab cakes are a popular appetizer, and this zesty recipe is my favorite way to prepare them. For those who prefer their seasoning on the mild side, the Cajun spices can be eliminated completely. These starters can also be served with a spicy mustard or tartar sauce.

6 slices white bread, crusts removed
2 eggs
1/4 cup heavy cream
1 tablespoon fresh lemon juice
1/2 teaspoon dry mustard
1 teaspoon Cajun spice mix (see Chef's Tip)
Salt to taste
1 teaspoon minced garlic
1 pound fresh or thawed frozen crabmeat, picked clean
4 green onions, finely chopped
4 strips smoked bacon, cooked crisp and crumbled
2 cups dried bread crumbs for coating
Vegetable oil for frying
Creole Honey-Mustard Sauce (recipe follows)

Tear up the bread slices and grind in a blender or food processor. Add the eggs, cream, and lemon juice to form a heavy batter, then remove to a bowl and add all the remaining ingredients except the dried bread crumbs, oil, and sauce.

Form into small cakes about 1 to 2 inches in diameter. Carefully coat them with the dried bread crumbs.

Heat a large skillet or sauté pan with 1/2 inch of vegetable oil over medium heat and fry some of the cakes until golden brown on both sides. Place in a 200°F oven to keep warm. Repeat until all cakes are fried. Serve warm with Creole honey-mustard sauce.

MAKES 24 CAKES; SERVES 12 AS APPETIZER

CHEF'S TIP: Cajun spice mix (usually containing oregano, paprika, cayenne, pepper, onion powder, and salt) can be purchased at the supermarket or mixed at home to suit your preference.

CREOLE HONEY-MUSTARD SAUCE

1 tablespoon vegetable oil
1 tablespoon crushed green peppercorns
1 tablespoon freshly ground pepper
1 shallot, minced
1/2 cup dry white wine
2 tablespoons Dijon mustard
2 tablespoons whole-grain mustard
6 tablespoons mayonnaise
6 tablespoons sour cream
1 tablespoon honey

In a small nonreactive saucepan over medium heat, heat the oil and sauté the peppercorns, pepper, and shallots for about 3 minutes, or until the shallots are translucent. Add the white wine and simmer until the wine has almost completely evaporated. Let cool. Add the remaining ingredients and check the seasoning.

MAKES ABOUT 1 1/2 CUPS

CHEF'S TIP: This dipping sauce will keep up to one week when stored covered in the refrigerator.

PUMPKIN-APPLE BISQUE IN JACK-O'-LANTERN BOWLS

CHEF KATHERINE SHEPARD: Pumpkin bisque is a terrific addition to any Halloween celebration. Kids enjoy eating this soup out of their own pumpkin "bowls." If small pumpkins aren't available, cut a large one to serve as a tureen. This soup is easily adapted to adult tastes with the addition of ¼ cup dry sherry just before serving.

8 small pumpkins (about 1 pound each)
⅓ cup plus 2 tablespoons unsalted butter
1 small onion, cut into ¼-inch dice
¼ cup all-purpose flour
6 cups milk or half-and-half, heated
1 bay leaf
One 29-ounce can pumpkin purée
Salt and freshly ground pepper to taste
1 apple peeled and cut into 1/8-inch dice
1 teaspoon fresh thyme leaves
1 pinch freshly grated or ground nutmeg
¼ cup dry sherry (optional)
1 cup heavy cream, whipped to soft peaks

Cut off the tops of the pumpkins and clean out the seeds and strings. Scoop out part of the pulp to form a clean cavity.

In a 4-quart heavy saucepan or stockpot, melt the ⅓ cup butter over medium heat and sauté onion until translucent, about 3 minutes. Add the flour and stir to form a paste. Cook and stir over low heat for 2 minutes.

Gradually whisk the warm milk or half-and-half into flour mixture. Add the bay leaf. Bring to a simmer and cook gently for 15 minutes. Add the pumpkin purée and simmer an additional 15 minutes over very low heat. Strain through doubled cheesecloth or pass through a food mill. Season with salt and pepper.

In a medium saucepan, melt the 2 tablespoons butter and sauté the apple for 2 minutes. Add the thyme and nutmeg and cook 2 to 3 minutes longer, or until the apple is tender but not mushy. Spoon a portion of apple into each carved pumpkin bowl.

Add the sherry, if using, to the hot soup and pour into the pumpkin bowls on top of the apples. Top with a dollop of whipped cream and serve.

SERVES 8

PARSNIP AND PARSLEY SOUP

CHEF FRITZ SONNENSCHMIDT, C.M.C.: This soup has been a family favorite for many generations, originating with my great-grandmother, a farmer, who passed it along to my grandmother, then to my mother, and myself. It is really a dish of necessity, since during the war in winter, these were the only ingredients we had. The soup was often the entire meal.

2 small bunches flat-leaf parsley, stemmed
3 to 4 bunches curly parsley, stemmed
2 cups chicken stock (page 38)
2 small parsnips, peeled and cut into julienne
4 tablespoons unsalted butter
2 shallots, chopped
1 clove garlic, minced
¼ teaspoon ground nutmeg
Juice of ½ lemon
Salt and freshly ground pepper to taste
⅓ cup heavy cream, lightly whipped

Bring a small saucepan of water to a boil. Blanch both kinds of parsley in the boiling water for 3 to 4 minutes. Drain and place in a bowl of ice water to stop the cooking. Drain again and squeeze out the excess moisture.

In a medium saucepan, bring the chicken stock to a simmer and add the julienned parsnips. Simmer for 10 to 15 minutes, drain, and set both the stock and parsnips aside.

In a stockpot over medium heat, melt the butter and sauté the shallots until translucent, about 2 minutes. Add the garlic and blanched parsley, reduce heat to low, and cook for 2 minutes. Add the stock and bring to a boil. Simmer for 3 to 5 minutes.

Using an immersion blender, or in batches in a blender or in a food processor, purée the contents of the stockpot. Season with the nutmeg, lemon juice, salt, and pepper. Fold in the lightly whipped cream until fully incorporated.

Serve the soup hot, with a scattering of the cooked parsnips on top.

SERVES 4

The vegetables i
suggestions. Feel
will not give the f
beets and beet gr
the stock foam ov
taste be your guid

2 teaspoons olive
1 to 2 garlic clove
2 teaspoons mince
8 cups water
½ cup dry white u
1 large onion, thin
1 leek, sliced
1 stalk celery, thin
1 carrot, peeled an
1 parsnip, thinly s
1 cup thinly sliced
1 cup sliced fennel
4 to 5 whole black
½ teaspoon juniper
1 bay leaf
1 sprig fresh thyme

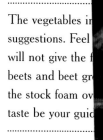

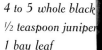

POTATO SOUP WITH MUSHROOMS AND MARJORAM

CHEF FRITZ SONNENSCHMIDT, C.M.C.: This recipe has been with me for nearly fifty years, and recalls fond memories of the master chef to whom I was apprenticed. She grew up on a farm, and this recipe was her favorite. It was a great honor when she allowed me to cook it for her, even though this made the other apprentices jealous!

2 tablespoons olive oil
8 ounces potatoes, peeled and cut into ¾-inch dice
1 onion, cut into ¼-inch dice
1 large leek (white part only), sliced
8 ounces mushrooms, sliced
1 tablespoon chopped fresh chervil
1 tablespoon chopped fresh marjoram
4 cups chicken stock (page 38)
Salt and freshly ground pepper, to taste
Ground nutmeg to taste
1 cup sour cream
2 tablespoons unsalted butter

In a large heavy saucepan over medium heat, heat the olive oil and sauté the potatoes and onion until golden, 5 to 7 minutes. Add the leek and mushrooms and cook 2 or 3 more minutes. Add half the chopped chervil and marjoram.

Add the chicken stock and simmer for 10 to 15 minutes, or until the potatoes are tender. Season with salt, pepper, and nutmeg. Purée in a blender or food processor until smooth. Stir in the sour cream and butter.

Sprinkle some of the remaining chervil and marjoram on top of each serving and serve hot.

SERVES 6

CHEF FRITZ Sc
a traditional c
my father-in-l
Pennsylvania, h
This soup is h
prepare it for
culinary delig

1 pound beef
8 cups beef st
2 tablespoons
1 onion, cut i
1 pound red b
2 tablespoons
½ teaspoon su
½ teaspoon so
1 cup shredde
1 small bay l
4 stems parsle
Salt and fresh
½ cup cubed
8 ounces kiell
4 teaspoons s
2 tablespoons

4 pounds chic
1 large onion,
1 carrot, peele
1 stalk celery,
5 to 6 whole
3 to 4 parsley
1 bay leaf
1 sprig fresh t

Place the

to 2 inches ab

medium heat,

Adjust the hea

Add all the re

face as necessa

Our Kwanzaa recipes are traditional dishes from Trinidad.

When the fall and early winter holidays are over, the start of a New Year brings many of us back to a commitment to better and healthier eating, and an annual vow to lose a few pounds! *Cooking Secrets of the CIA* recognizes that the traditionally heartier foods of fall and winter should be balanced after the holidays with foods that are luscious and low in fat, and we have provided recipes that offer that balance.

One truly American tradition is the Superbowl and, of course, the halftime Superbowl party. We have included dishes that are sure to please a crowd of gridiron spectators.

St. Valentine's Day immediately conjures up images of chocolates, flowers, and lovers' promises. Valentine was a Christian priest who was martyred by the Roman emperor in A.D. 270. As legend has it, he secretly married hundreds of young couples in Rome before being beheaded. February 14, the day of Valentine's death, is named after him in recognition of his efforts to unite young lovers; fittingly, our Valentine's Day entrée has at least one successful marriage proposal associated with it!

The anticipation of the New Year causes rejoicing in Asian countries. The lunar New Year has great emotional and religious significance and is celebrated with pomp and tradition both in Asia and America.

Centuries ago, the Chinese began preparing for the New Year as much as a month in advance by cleansing both their homes and their spirits. Debts were settled, homes were cleaned and repaired, and families were reunited. The kitchen god, usually represented by a small figurine, was dusted off and fed a final dinner of sweets, so that he would speak well of his owners in the next world. The god was set on fire and ascended to the heavens in the form of smoke.

On the last day of the old year, a new kitchen god was bought, an enormous feast was prepared, and all knives were put away for 24 hours, so that no one could cut "good luck" accidentally before the New Year. The door to the home was sealed, and a ritual of prayers and offerings to ancestors was begun. At midnight, the children of the home broke the seal on the door to let good luck and the New Year in.

While today's Chinese celebrations vary from this historical accounting, the New Year is still the most prominent Chinese holiday. Firecrackers, parades, gift-giving and, of course, ceremonial foods make up the festivities. Our menu in honor of the Chinese New Year features a Mongolian hot pot, and steamed dumplings for good luck.

GAMBERI CON INSALATA DI FAGIOLI
(SHRIMP WITH WARM BEAN SALAD)

CHEF JOSEPH DIPERRI: The authentic way to prepare this dish is with the heads left on the shrimp. It is customary for guests to remove the heads and suck out the juices.

20 extra-large shrimp, with heads on
¼ cup olive oil
1 small onion, cut into ¼-inch dice
2 cloves garlic, minced
5 tomatoes, seeded and cut into eighths (see Chef's Tip)
1 teaspoon red pepper flakes
1 bay leaf
1 cup dry white wine
2 cups shrimp stock (recipe follows) or chicken stock (page 38)
Salt to taste
Warm Bean Salad (recipe follows)

Peel and devein the shrimp. Reserve the shells for making stock.

In a large sauté pan over medium heat, heat the olive oil and sauté the shrimp until the heads turn pink and the flesh turns white, about 2 minutes. Remove the shrimp from the pan with a slotted spoon. Add the onion and garlic to the pan and sauté until translucent, about 2 to 3 minutes. Add the tomatoes, pepper flakes, and bay leaf. Cook until the tomatoes are tender. Add the wine and stock and cook to reduce by one fourth. Return the shrimp to the pan and cook until they are firm, 1 or 2 minutes. Season with salt.

Serve immediately with the warm bean salad.

SERVES 4 TO 6

CHEF'S TIP: If canned tomatoes must be used, use whole plum (Roma) tomatoes.

COLUMBUS DAY: AN ITALIAN FEAST

SHRIMP STOCK

CHEF JOSEPH DIPERRI: This flavorful stock can be used in almost any seafood dish, and is even more pronounced when made with fish stock. It will keep in the refrigerator for 3 to 4 days. You may also freeze it for future use.

2 tablespoons olive oil
2 cups shrimp shells (from about 20 extra-large shrimp)
1 onion, cut into ¾-inch dice
1 stalk celery, coarsely chopped
1 carrot, peeled and coarsely chopped
1 tablespoon tomato paste
3 tablespoons brandy
3 cups chicken stock (page 38) or fish stock
Salt and freshly ground pepper to taste

In a large sauté pan over medium-low heat, heat the oil and sauté the shells until they turn pink. Add the onion, celery, carrot, and tomato paste. Mix well and continue cooking until the liquid has evaporated and the vegetables have caramelized, about 5 minutes.

Add the brandy and ignite, using a lighted bamboo skewer. When the flame goes out, add the stock and slowly simmer for 25 minutes. Pass through a fine-meshed sieve. Season with salt and pepper.

MAKES ABOUT 2 CUPS

WARM BEAN SALAD

CHEF JOSEPH DIPERRI: This versatile salad goes well with shrimp. It can also form the base for the popular soup pasta fagioli.

½ cup dried white navy beans
½ cup dried cranberry beans
¼ cup olive oil
6 ounces pancetta, cut into ¼-inch dice
1 small onion, minced
1 to 2 stems each fresh rosemary, marjoram, thyme, and parsley
1 clove garlic, minced
3 cups chicken stock (page 38)

Soak the beans overnight in water to cover.

In a large, heavy saucepan over medium heat, heat the olive oil and cook the pancetta until golden brown. Add the onion and sauté until translucent, about 3 minutes.

Tie the fresh herbs into a bundle with cotton string. Add the drained beans, herbs, garlic, and stock to the saucepan and simmer slowly until the beans are tender, about 45 minutes to 1 hour.

Remove the herbs. Let the beans cool a little and serve warm.

SERVES 4 TO 6

CHEF'S TIP: If canned beans are used, drain them before using and be careful not to overcook.

COLUMBUS DAY: A SPANISH MEAL
PAELLA VALENCIANA

CHEF JOSEBA ENCABO: The Spanish embrace this as their national dish and endorse many regional variations. This version uses short-grain rice from the Valencia region. The seafood must always be fresh and, ideally, locally caught. If there is one unique attribute to true paella, it is the use of only one seasoning: saffron. Nothing else is needed or used to flavor this complete one-dish meal.

6 cups chicken stock (page 38)
1 cup tomato sauce
1 tablespoon saffron threads
Salt to taste
¼ cup extra-virgin olive oil
1 pound boneless chicken meat, skinned and cut into 1-inch cubes
½ pound chorizo, cut into ½-inch pieces
1 pound boneless pork or beef, cut into 1-inch cubes
2 yellow onions, cut into ⅓-inch dice
1 green bell pepper, seeded, deribbed, and cut into ⅓-inch dice
1 red bell pepper, seeded, deribbed, and cut into ⅓-inch dice

3 carrots, peeled and cut into ¼-inch dice
3 cloves garlic, minced
3 cups short-grain rice, preferably Spanish
1 cup green peas
10 mussels in shells
10 clams in shells
10 large shrimp in shells with tails and heads intact
4 lemons
2 red bell peppers, roasted (see Chef's Tips), peeled, seeded, and cut into ¼-inch strips

Heat the chicken stock, tomato sauce, saffron, and salt in a large saucepan over medium heat. In a paella pan over medium-high heat, heat the oil and sauté the chicken, chorizo, and pork or beef until well browned, about 3 to 5 minutes. Add the onions, diced bell peppers, carrots, and garlic and sauté for about 2 more minutes. Add the rice and stir to coat it slightly with the rest of

(recipe continues)

the ingredients. Add the stock mixture and stir. Taste and adjust the seasoning. Bring to a simmer and cook for 8 minutes.

Add the peas, mussels, clams, and shrimp to the paella pan, arranging the shellfish in a pattern, if desired. Add more stock if the previous amount has all been absorbed. Continue cooking at a simmer until the clams and mussels have opened, about 5 more minutes. (Discard any that do not open.)

Remove from the heat, squeeze 2 of the lemons over the top, cover, and let sit for 5 minutes. Garnish with the roasted peppers and the remaining 2 lemons, cut into wedges.

SERVES 10

CHEF'S TIPS: You may substitute a skillet, large frying pan, or other shallow pan for the paella pan.

Roasted peppers are available in most food markets in cans or jars. If you want to roast your own, begin by brushing the whole peppers with olive oil. Place in a preheated 350°F oven on a baking sheet and roast for about 30 to 45 minutes, or until the skin blisters and turns black. (Alternatively, put the peppers on top of a grill or under a broiler, turning occasionally.) Place the pepper in a paper or plastic bag to steam for 5 minutes. Remove from the bag and peel by hand. Remove the stem and seeds and cut as desired.

A TRADITIONAL THANKSGIVING DINNER

Roast Turkey with Pan Sauce ➤ *Bread Dressing*
Succotash ➤ *Candied Sweet Potatoes* ➤ *Squash Turbans*

ROAST TURKEY WITH PAN SAUCE

CHEF TIMOTHY RYAN, C.M.C.: No meal is more eagerly anticipated or more thoroughly enjoyed by most Americans than the traditional Thanksgiving Day feast of roast turkey, bread stuffing, cranberries, and all the accompaniments. While the "trimmings" may vary a bit from family to family, various squashes, corn, and sweet potatoes have likely been a part of the Thanksgiving menu since the Pilgrims' very first feast. Here, the meal is intended for a gathering of 6 people, although the turkey will produce enough for 10—I like to plan on having leftover turkey to enjoy for several days after Thanksgiving.

½ cup (1 stick) unsalted butter
One 15-pound turkey
Salt and freshly ground pepper, to taste
1 bay leaf
1 large sprig fresh thyme
Stems from ½ bunch fresh flat-leaf parsley
5 to 7 tablespoons arrowroot
About 5 cups chicken stock (page 38)
Bread Dressing (recipe follows)

Preheat the oven to 450°F. Melt the butter in a small saucepan, then let it cool at room temperature without solidifying. While the butter is cooling, season the cavity of the turkey with salt and pepper. Place the bay leaf, thyme, and parsley inside the cavity and truss the turkey. Brush butter over the entire bird, then sprinkle with salt and pepper.

Place the turkey in a roasting pan, put into the preheated oven, and immediately reduce the oven temperature to 350°F.

Roast the bird for 3 hours and 45 minutes to 5 hours, or until a thermometer inserted in the thigh and *not* touching bone registers 165°F. Transfer the bird to a platter and let it rest for about 30 minutes before carving; the bird will continue to cook during this time.

While the turkey is resting, prepare the sauce. Dissolve the arrowroot in 1 cup of the stock. Pour the fat and juices from the roasting pan into a container. Let the juices settle to the bottom and spoon off the fat.

Place the roasting pan on top of the stove over medium heat. Add the juices back to the pan along with the remaining 4 cups chicken stock (about ¼ cup for every pound of turkey). Bring the liquid to a boil, scraping the bottom of the pan to release the browned drippings on the bottom. Thicken the sauce by whisking in the arrowroot diluted with stock.

When the sauce returns to a boil, reduce heat and let simmer for 5 to 10 minutes. Adjust the seasoning and strain through a sieve. The sauce is now ready to serve.

Carve the turkey and spoon the sauce over each portion, or serve the sauce on the side for guests to help themselves. Serve with bread dressing.

SERVES 10

CHEF'S TIP: Here are some general rules to help plan how long a turkey should roast. Note: All guidelines are for *unstuffed* birds. The CIA does not recommend stuffing your turkey.

➤ Up to 6 pounds: 20 minutes per pound

➤ 6 to 16 pounds: 15 to 20 minutes per pound

➤ Over 16 pounds: 13 to 15 minutes per pound

HANUKKAH DISHES

Atlantic Salmon in a Potato Crust with Chive Oil and Leek Purée
Braised Brisket with Red Wine ➤ *Potato Latkes*

ATLANTIC SALMON IN A POTATO CRUST WITH CHIVE OIL AND LEEK PURÉE

CHEF MOREY KANNER: Salmon is a flavorful fish that works well with simple accompaniments, such as this potato crust and leek purée. I recommend serving this with a mixture of lima beans and julienned tomatoes heated in a small amount of chicken broth. The chive oil is quite flavorful, and symbolizes the oil that lighted the holy temple lamp during the eight nights of the first Hanukkah.

4 salmon fillets (4 to 5 ounces each), skin on
1 Idaho potato, peeled and cut into julienne
Salt and freshly ground pepper to taste
Vegetable oil for frying
1 tablespoon olive oil plus ½ cup
3 leeks (white part only), sliced
½ cup chicken stock (page 38)
2 tablespoons fresh lemon juice
1 bunch fresh chives

Season the salmon and potato with salt and pepper. Pack a thin layer of potatoes on the flesh side of each salmon fillet.

Add enough vegetable oil to liberally cover the bottom of a 10-inch skillet or sauté pan. Place over medium-high heat. When wisps of smoke begin to rise from the oil, place the salmon fillets, potato-side down, into the oil. Fry 3 to 5 minutes until golden brown, then gently turn over. Cook another 2 to 3 minutes until salmon is firm but slightly springy to the touch. Remove and keep warm.

In a large, heavy saucepan, heat the 1 tablespoon olive oil and sauté the leeks until translucent, about 3 minutes. Add the stock and simmer until tender. Transfer to a blender and purée the leeks and stock. Pass through a fine-meshed sieve. Adjust the seasoning with lemon juice, salt, and pepper. Set aside and keep warm.

In a clean blender, purée the chives with the ½ cup olive oil. Allow to settle, then strain.

To serve, put a portion of the leek purée in the center of each plate, top with a salmon fillet, potato-crust side up, and drizzle chive oil over the fish.

SERVES 4

BRAISED BRISKET WITH RED WINE

CHEF MOREY KANNER: The key to the brisket is the marinade, and a handy way to marinate it is to place the meat in a large self-sealing plastic bag. Pour in the marinade and seal the bag. Turn the bag a few times to thoroughly coat the meat.

3 to 4 pounds beef brisket, trimmed of all fat
2 cups dry red wine
4 cloves garlic, minced
1 small onion, cut into ¼-inch dice
2 carrots, peeled and cut into ¼-inch dice
2 stalks celery, cut into ¼-inch dice
1 teaspoon peppercorns
1 teaspoon fresh thyme leaves
2 tablespoons vegetable oil
¼ cup ketchup
3 cups beef stock

Place the brisket in a plastic bag (see introductory note) or a large glass bowl. In another bowl, combine the wine, garlic, onion, carrots, celery, peppercorns, and thyme. Pour the mixture over the brisket, cover or seal, and marinate in the refrigerator for 8 hours.

Preheat the oven to 350°F. Drain the marinade from the beef and reserve half of it. Pat the beef dry with paper towels.

In a large, heavy flameproof casserole or Dutch oven, heat the vegetable oil over high heat until wisps of smoke appear. Place the brisket in the pan and sear on all sides, then transfer to a plate.

Pour off the fat from the cooking pan, add the ketchup, and cook over medium-low heat until a rust color develops, 3 to 4 minutes. Add the reserved marinade and scrape up the browned drippings on the bottom of the pan with a wooden spoon. Return the brisket to the pan and add the stock (the braising liquid should be about one third of the way up the side of the brisket).

Bring to a simmer, cover, and braise in the oven until the meat is fork tender, about 1½ hours. Remove the brisket and keep warm.

Skim the excess grease from the cooking liquid. Purée the liquid in a blender. If it is too thick, thin with stock; if too thin, cook down until thickened.

Slice the brisket and serve warm with the sauce.

SERVES 8 TO 10

CHEF'S TIP: If you use canned beef broth in this recipe, make sure it is a low-salt variety.

HANUKKAH DISHES
POTATO LATKES

CHEF MOREY KANNER: I learned this classic Jewish recipe from my grandmother. She would often grate the potatoes ahead of time and keep them in water until ready to use. Then they need only be squeezed out. The water that comes out of the potatoes can be left standing until all of the starch settles to the bottom. This can be used in the latkes instead of flour, by pouring off the clear water until you reach the cloudy starch.

4 large Idaho potatoes, peeled
1 small onion
2 eggs, beaten
¼ cup matzo meal
2 to 3 tablespoons all-purpose flour
1 teaspoon salt
¼ teaspoon freshly ground pepper
Vegetable oil for frying
Sour cream and applesauce for serving

Coarsely grate the potatoes and onion on a box grater. Squeeze the excess moisture from the potato mixture and place in a large bowl. Add the beaten eggs, matzo, and flour and combine. Let stand 10 minutes so the matzo absorbs all of the moisture. Season with salt and pepper.

Add about ¼ inch of oil to a large skillet or sauté pan and place over medium-high heat, to about 350°F (see Chef's Tips). Form the latkes into cakes 2½ inches in diameter. Fry a batch of latkes 2 to 3 minutes on both sides until golden brown and crisp. Drain on paper towels and keep warm in a 200°F oven. Repeat until all the latkes are cooked. Serve with sour cream and applesauce.

MAKES 20 PANCAKES; SERVES 8 TO 10

CHEF'S TIPS: Alternate grating each potato with some onion so that the acid of the onion helps to slow the oxidation of the potato.

To determine when the oil has reached about 350°F, look for a slightly shimmering surface. Test by adding a small amount of the latke mixture; there should be moderate bubbling as the latke fries.

VARIATIONS: Add to the mixture before frying:

➤ 1 leek (white part only) cleaned, diced, and sautéed in 1 teaspoon vegetable oil until translucent

➤ 4 ounces chopped smoked salmon trimmings and 2 table-spoons chopped green onions or fresh chives

A CHRISTMAS FEAST

Roast Goose with Apple-Prune Sauce
Bread and Giblet Dumplings ➤ *Glazed Root Vegetables*

ROAST GOOSE WITH APPLE-PRUNE SAUCE

CHEF JOSEPH WEISSENBERG: The tradition of a Christmas goose dinner is a longstanding one. Every part of the goose is used here, from the giblets in the dumplings to the wings and neck added to the sauce. Along with no waste comes a well-flavored meal.

1 fresh or thawed frozen goose, 10 to 12 pounds
Salt and freshly ground pepper to taste
1 Golden Delicious apple, peeled, cored, and cut into ¼-inch dice
8 pitted prunes
One 2- to 3-inch sprig fresh rosemary
1 small carrot, peeled and coarsely chopped
1 onion, coarsely chopped
1 stalk celery, coarsely chopped

Preheat the oven to 350°F. Reserve the goose wings, neck, gizzard, and liver for sauce. Prick the skin of the goose with the tip of a knife in several places. Season with salt and pepper.

Insert the diced apple into the body cavity with the prunes and rosemary. Truss the goose and place it on its side on a rack in a roasting pan. Roast for 30 minutes, then turn the goose over and roast 30 minutes longer. Remove from the pan and pour out the excess fat, reserving it for the sauce and dumplings.

Return the goose to the pan, breast-side up, and turn the

oven down to 325°F. Continue to roast 1½ hours longer or until a meat thermometer inserted in a thigh registers 165°F.

While the goose is roasting, put 2 tablespoons of the reserved fat in a medium-heavy saucepan and heat over medium heat. Cut the wings and neck into 2-inch pieces and add to the hot fat along with the gizzard. Brown lightly. Add the carrot, onion, and celery. Brown and add water to cover. Bring to a boil, reduce the heat, and simmer, uncovered, for 1 hour. Add the liver and continue to simmer for 15 minutes longer. Strain and reserve the meat pieces for use in the dumplings. Reserve the remaining liquid to use as stock.

Remove the goose from the roasting pan and keep warm. Pour off the fat from the roasting pan. Pour in the reserved stock, bring to a boil, and stir to scrape up the browned bits from the bottom of the pan. Strain and let cool to room temperature.

Remove the apples and prunes from the goose and place in a blender with the cooled pan sauce. Blend to a purée and season to taste with salt and pepper. Place in a saucepan and heat quickly while you carve the goose. Serve the sliced goose with the sauce.

SERVES 8 TO 10

A CHRISTMAS FEAST
BREAD AND GIBLET DUMPLINGS

2 tablespoons goose fat (rendered from roast goose)
1 large onion, cut into ⅛-inch dice
Liver, gizzards, and neck meat from goose, cut into ⅛-inch dice
2 pounds day-old French bread, cut into ½-inch dice
1¼ cups all-purpose flour
2 tablespoons chopped fresh flat-leaf parsley
10 large eggs
2 cups milk
¼ teaspoon ground white pepper
2 teaspoons poultry seasoning

In a medium sauté pan, heat the goose fat and sauté the onion until translucent, about 3 to 4 minutes. Add the diced goose giblets and meat, toss, and allow to cool.

In a large bowl, mix the bread cubes, flour, and parsley. In another bowl, beat the eggs and add the milk, pepper, and poultry seasoning. Pour over the bread cubes and mix well. Blend in the onion and diced giblets and meat. Cover and allow to rest for 1 hour.

Bring a large pot of water to a boil. Wet your hands and form the bread mixture into balls about 2 inches in diameter. Drop into the rapidly boiling water, cover, and reduce heat. Simmer for 10 minutes, uncover, and simmer 5 minutes longer.

MAKES 20 DUMPLINGS; SERVES 8 TO 10

GLAZED ROOT VEGETABLES

2 cups chicken stock (page 38)
1 pound carrots, peeled and cut into ¾-inch dice
1 pound rutabagas, peeled and cut into ¾-inch dice
1 pound turnips, peeled and cut into ¾-inch dice
1 pound parsnips, peeled and cut into ¾-inch dice
4 tablespoons unsalted butter
1 tablespoon chopped fresh flat-leaf parsley
Salt and freshly ground pepper, to taste

Bring the stock to a boil in a large saucepan. Add the carrots and rutabagas and cook for 4 or 5 minutes. Add the turnips and parsnips and cook until the vegetables are tender, about 4 or 5 minutes. Remove all the vegetables from the stock, place in a serving dish, and keep warm.

Boil the chicken stock, uncovered, over high heat until reduced by about one third. Remove from the heat and stir in the butter. Add the parsley, salt, and pepper.

Pour over the warm vegetables and serve.

SERVES 8 TO 10

KWANZAA DISHES

The Cameron Queen's Stewed Chicken with Pigeon Peas
Matura Beef Pilau

THE CAMERON QUEEN'S STEWED CHICKEN WITH PIGEON PEAS

CHEF FRANK LOPEZ: This recipe's unique name is a tribute to my mother. She was regarded as the "queen" of Cameron, Trinidad, because of her delicious cooking, particularly this dish. This is the perfect selection for Kwanzaa celebrations, as pigeon peas are fresh right around the end of December. If you can't find fresh pigeon peas, canned and dried ones are usually available all year long.

2 chickens (about 3 pounds each), cut into 2-inch pieces
Juice of 2 lemons
1 teaspoon salt
½ teaspoon freshly ground pepper
4 small onions
1 bay leaf
2 whole cloves
3 tablespoons vegetable oil
4 tablespoons sugar
4 cloves garlic, crushed
2 carrots, peeled and cut into ⅓-inch dice

2 stalks celery, cut into ⅓-inch dice
2 green bell peppers, seeded, deribbed, and cut into ⅓-inch dice
2 red bell peppers, seeded, deribbed, and cut into ⅓-inch dice
4 tomatoes, seeded and cut into ⅓-inch dice
½ teaspoon chopped fresh thyme leaves
2 tablespoons chopped fresh flat-leaf parsley
1 teaspoon finely chopped fresh ginger
½ cup water
2 cans (16 ounces) pigeon peas
8 cups steamed white rice for serving

Place the chicken in a shallow glass bowl and sprinkle with lemon juice, salt, and pepper. Cover and marinate for 20 to 30 minutes.

Cut 3 of the onions into ⅓-inch dice. Attach the bay leaf to the fourth onion by pushing the pointed ends of the cloves through the bay leaf and into the onion. (In this way the whole cloves and bay leaf can be removed easily from the stew before serving.)

(recipe continues)

In a large, heavy flameproof casserole or Dutch oven, heat the oil over high heat. Add the sugar and heat, without stirring, until melted and browned. Drain the chicken pieces, add to the casserole, and cover. Stir after 2 minutes, lower heat to medium, and add the garlic and diced onions. Cook 5 minutes more, or until the chicken is fully browned.

Add the diced carrot, celery, bell peppers, and tomatoes and simmer 2 to 3 minutes, stirring occasionally. Add the onion studded with the bay leaf and cloves, the thyme, parsley, ginger, and water. Simmer for 5 minutes. Add the peas with their liquid and bring to a boil. Lower the heat and simmer very slowly until chicken is tender, about 20 to 30 minutes.

Remove the studded onion and serve the chicken and sauce with steamed white rice.

SERVES 8

chop it. Add the rock shrimp to the pan and cook over medium heat for 2 to 3 minutes. Add the pasta and chopped clams. Heat until the pasta is warmed through, stir in the pesto, season with salt and pepper, and serve.

SERVES 10

CHEF'S TIP: Canned chopped clams in juice may be substituted for fresh clams in this recipe.

REDUCED-FAT PESTO

3½ cups loosely packed basil leaves
About ½ cup pine nuts, lightly toasted (see Chef's Tips)
2 tablespoons olive oil
½ cup freshly grated Parmesan cheese
1 clove garlic, minced
Water as needed

Combine all the ingredients except the water in a blender or food processor and purée to a coarse paste. With the motor running, add water, a little at a time, until a smooth paste forms. Use immediately or cover and refrigerate.

MAKES ABOUT 1¼ CUPS

CHEF'S TIPS: Pesto may be stored up to a month in the refrigerator, and up to 6 months in the freezer.

Toast pine nuts by placing them in a cast-iron skillet or on a baking sheet in a 350°F oven for 5 to 7 minutes. Stir occasionally to insure even coloring. Remove from oven as soon as they begin to turn a light brown.

ROASTED-VEGETABLE BABY PIZZAS

CATHARINE H. POWERS, M.S., R.D., CHEF DAVID ST. JOHN-GRUBB: We think of pizza dough as a plate or platter for a variety of favorite toppings. This is a contemporary version of the medieval trencher. While pizza dough can be made from scratch, most pizzerias will be happy to sell you fresh dough.

2 tablespoons olive oil

4 cloves garlic, peeled

1 onion, peeled

1 leek (white part only)

2 beets, peeled

2 carrots, peeled

2 parsnips, peeled

¼ bulb fennel, cored and quartered

Olive oil for coating

12 ounces pizza dough (see Chef's Tip)

½ teaspoon salt

½ teaspoon freshly ground pepper

1 teaspoon chopped fresh dill

4 ounces goat cheese, crumbled (about ¾ cup)

Preheat the oven to 350°F. Coat the vegetables with olive oil. Place in a terra-cotta vegetable roaster or other large roasting pan, cover, and bake until tender, about 45 minutes. Remove the vegetables from the oven and raise the temperature to 450°F. When vegetables are cool enough to handle, cut them into julienne.

Divide the pizza dough into 4 equal balls. On a lightly floured surface, press the dough by hand into disks about 8 inches in diameter. Transfer to lightly oiled baking pans. Divide the roasted vegetables equally among the pizzas. Season with salt, pepper, and dill. Top with goat cheese.

Bake until the pizza dough is browned, about 10 minutes. Serve immediately.

MAKES 4 INDIVIDUAL PIZZAS

CHEF'S TIP: If you want to make your own pizza dough, use the recipe for focaccia on page 26.

VEGETABLE COUSCOUS

CATHARINE H. POWERS, M.S., R.D., CHEF DAVID ST. JOHN-GRUBB: Seven is considered by many to be a lucky number—hence the seven vegetables used in this nontraditional couscous. Typically, a pan called a *couscoussiere* is used for the steaming of the couscous grain; however, in this version we simplified the preparation.

8¾ cups vegetable stock (page 39)
½ teaspoon ground turmeric
1 teaspoon curry powder
½ cup chickpeas, soaked overnight in water to cover and drained
3 carrots, peeled and sliced on the diagonal
½ cup pearl onions, peeled, boiled for 4 minutes, cooled
2 artichoke hearts, quartered
1 zucchini, cut into ¾-inch dice
1 tomato, peeled, seeded, and cut into ¼-inch dice (see page 98)
1 cup packed spinach leaves
½ teaspoon freshly grated nutmeg
Pinch saffron threads
2 cups couscous
½ cup raisins, blanched for 2 minutes, drained, cooled
¼ cup sliced almonds, toasted (see Chef's Tips)
Harissa (see Chef's Tips)

In a medium saucepan, blend 4 cups of the vegetable stock with the turmeric and curry powder. Add the soaked chickpeas, bring to a simmer, and cook for 2 to 2½ hours. Drain and set aside.

In a medium sauté pan, heat ¼ cup of the stock over medium heat and cook the carrots and onions, covered, for 4 minutes.

Add the artichokes and cook 2 minutes longer. Set aside and keep warm.

Add ¼ cup of the stock to the pan with the zucchini and tomato and cook them, covered, over medium heat for 4 to 5 minutes. Set aside and keep warm.

Add ¼ cup of the stock to the pan with the spinach and sprinkle in the nutmeg. Sauté over medium heat to wilt the spinach, about 1 to 2 minutes. Set aside and keep warm.

Bring the remaining 4 cups stock to a boil in a medium saucepan, remove from heat, and steep the saffron in it for 5 minutes. Add the couscous, return the stock to a boil, cover, and remove from heat. Let sit for 5 to 6 minutes. Stir with a fork.

To serve, place the couscous in the center of a platter or plates. Arrange the vegetables around it. Garnish with raisins and almonds. Drizzle with a little harissa.

SERVES 4

CHEF'S TIPS: To toast almonds, place them in a cast-iron skillet in a 350°F oven and bake, stirring occasionally, until golden, about 8 minutes.

Harissa is a hot pepper sauce available in most gourmet shops and Middle Eastern groceries.

JERUSALEM ARTICHOKE, SPINACH, AND RICOTTA TART WITH A WILD RICE CRUST

CATHARINE H. POWERS, M.S., R.D., CHEF DAVID ST. JOHN-GRUBB: The USDA Food Guide Pyramid encourages Americans to base their diet on grains, cereals, fruits, and vegetables, and to exercise moderation when consuming meat and dairy products. This recipe is a creative and flavorful way to follow the pyramid guidelines and still "wow" your dining companions. Although wild rice is the grain used here, other grains can be substituted or added to the crust.

WILD RICE CRUST
4 cups wild rice
1 teaspoon salt
¾ cup sesame seeds, toasted (see Chef's Tip)
2 to 3 tablespoons tahini (sesame paste)
¾ cup whole-wheat flour or corn flour
3 to 4 teaspoons soy sauce

FILLING
1 tablespoon olive oil
2 cloves garlic, minced
3 cups spinach leaves
⅛ teaspoon freshly grated nutmeg
1 cup sliced and peeled Jerusalem artichokes
1 cup grated carrots
1 cup sliced onions
1 cup ricotta cheese

3 large egg whites, beaten lightly
1 tablespoon fresh marjoram, or 1 teaspoon dried marjoram
½ teaspoon salt
¼ teaspoon freshly ground pepper
⅓ cup freshly grated Parmesan cheese

Dressed mixed greens for garnish

To make the crust: Place the wild rice and salt in a 2-quart saucepan and add water to 2 inches above the rice. Bring to a light simmer and cook, uncovered, until all the liquid is absorbed, about 1 hour.

Preheat the oven to 375° F. In a large bowl, combine the cooked wild rice with all the remaining crust ingredients and mix well. Adjust the seasonings. Press into a well-oiled 12-inch tart or quiche pan. Cover with plastic wrap and chill while preparing the filling.

To make the filling: In a medium sauté pan, heat the olive oil over medium heat and sauté the garlic until it is golden. Add the spinach and toss it in the warm pan to wilt, about 2 minutes;

(recipe continues)

POST-HOLIDAY DISHES: LUSCIOUS AND LIGHT

season with nutmeg. Remove the spinach from the pan and drain away excess moisture. Layer the spinach and garlic mixture on the wild rice crust. In a bowl, combine the Jerusalem artichokes, carrots, and onions, then layer them over the spinach and garlic. Blend the ricotta, egg whites, and marjoram. Season with the salt and pepper. Pour over the vegetables carefully. Dust with the Parmesan cheese. Bake in the bottom third of the oven until the crust is golden and the filling is set, about 20 minutes.

Unmold the pie and place in the center of a plate. Garnish with a small bouquet of dressed mixed greens. Cut the pie into wedges to serve.

SERVES 6

CHEF'S TIP: Toast sesame seeds by placing them in a cast iron skillet or on a baking sheet and baking in a 350°F oven for 5 to 7 minutes until golden brown. Stir occasionally to insure even coloring.

SUPERBOWL SUNDAY DISHES

New Mexico–Style Green Chili and Pork Stew with Potatoes
Tangy Orange Barbecued Shrimp with Bacon on a Bed of Jícama and Sweet Red Pepper Salad

NEW MEXICO–STYLE GREEN CHILI AND PORK STEW WITH POTATOES

CHEF JIM HEYWOOD: I have won numerous state chili championships with my extra-secret, never-shared chili recipe. However, I did manage to snatch this recipe from a competitor in New Mexico, and I think it's a great version of chili. Once you're hooked, you may find yourself making your own version of chili—and you'll understand why I won't give mine away!

2 tablespoons vegetable oil or more as needed

3 pounds boneless lean pork, cut into ½ to ¾-inch cubes

2 large onions, cut into medium dice

5 cloves garlic, finely minced

4 cups chicken stock (page 38)

¼ cup tomato purée

3 to 9 poblano chilies, roasted, seeded, peeled, and cut into
    ½-inch pieces (page 59)

1 tablespoon ground cumin

2 teaspoons ground Mexican oregano (see Chef's Tips)

2 tablespoons mild red chili powder

2 jalapeño chilies, seeded and finely minced

2 tablespoons green Tabasco sauce (see Chef's Tips)

1 teaspoon distilled white vinegar

2 teaspoons salt

5 to 6 unpeeled Red Bliss potatoes or other red boiling potatoes,
    cut into ½-inch pieces

Warm flour tortillas and grated Monterey jack cheese for serving

Heat the 2 tablespoons vegetable oil in a large sauté pan over medium heat. Add the pork and sauté until gray. Remove from the pan and place in a 4-quart heavy saucepan. Sauté the onions and garlic in the same pan, using a little more oil if needed. Add the cooked onions and garlic, stock, tomato purée, poblanos, cumin, oregano, and chili powder. Bring the mixture to a boil, reduce the heat to a simmer, and cook, covered, for 1 hour, stirring occasionally.

Add the jalapeños, Tabasco, vinegar, salt, and potatoes. Cook, covered, at a simmer, for about 20 minutes, or until the potatoes are tender.

Serve in bowls, accompanied with warm flour tortillas and grated Monterey jack cheese.

SERVES 10

CHEF'S TIPS: Mexican oregano is available in Latino markets and the Tex-Mex section of most groceries.

Green Tabasco, new to the market, is milder in flavor than traditional Tabasco, as it is made from jalapeños.

SUPERBOWL SUNDAY DISHES

TANGY ORANGE BARBECUED SHRIMP WITH BACON ON A BED OF JÍCAMA AND SWEET RED PEPPER SALAD

CHEF JIM HEYWOOD: When the CIA opened the American Bounty Restaurant in 1982, this quickly became one of our most popular menu items. The combination of shrimp, crisp bacon, and a zesty barbecue sauce make for a tantalizing appetizer to a chili dinner, or a great entrée when paired with a salad. The barbecue sauce recipe makes 2 cups and can also be used as a basting sauce for ribs, chicken, or lamb.

TANGY ORANGE BARBECUE SAUCE

¾ cup (6-ounce can) frozen orange juice concentrate, thawed
¾ cup chili sauce
⅓ cup molasses
3 tablespoons soy sauce
1 tablespoon dark brown mustard
1 clove garlic, mashed
2 tablespoons fresh lemon juice
¼ cup chicken stock (page 38)
1 teaspoon Tabasco sauce
1 teaspoon salt
2 teaspoons Worcestershire sauce

10 strips smoked bacon
20 extra-large shrimp, peeled and deveined
Jícama and Sweet Red Pepper Salad (recipe follows)

To make the barbecue sauce: Combine all the ingredients in a medium bowl and mix well. Place in a medium saucepan, cover, and simmer gently for 20 minutes. Stir occasionally and be careful not to scorch. Cool, cover, and refrigerate.

Preheat the broiler and line a baking sheet with aluminum foil. In a large skillet or sauté pan over medium heat, cook the bacon until the fat is translucent. Drain on paper towels and cut each strip in half crosswise. Wrap each shrimp with one piece of the bacon. Secure with a toothpick and place on a wire rack. Place the rack on the prepared tray and broil the shrimp until the bacon is crisp. Turn the shrimp over and broil until the other side is crisp. Set the oven temperature at 500°F. Baste both sides of the shrimp with barbecue sauce and place in the oven for 2 minutes. Turn the shrimp over and return to the oven for 3 to 6 minutes longer, or until the shrimp are pink and opaque.

To serve, arrange a bed of jícama and sweet red pepper salad on 10 small plates and place 2 shrimp on top of each.

SERVES 10

CHEF'S TIPS: These shrimp work well as an appetizer or as a light meal, served with a salad, corn bread or garlic toast, and a mug of cold beer. They can also be served at a large party or buffet by arranging all of the shrimp on a platter by themselves or on a bed of salad.

The barbecue sauce may be kept in the refrigerator for up to one week. If stored in the freezer it will keep for up to six months.

JÍCAMA AND SWEET RED PEPPER SALAD

Juice of 1 lemon
1 tablespoon sugar
1½ teaspoons salt
1 teaspoon Tabasco sauce
⅓ cup vegetable oil
1 pound jícama, peeled and julienned
1 large red bell pepper, seeded, deribbed, and cut into julienne
2 cloves garlic, minced
2 tablespoons chopped fresh cilantro
2 green onions sliced thin on the bias

In a salad bowl, blend the lemon juice with the sugar, salt, and Tabasco sauce. Whisk in oil in a steady stream. Toss the jícama and bell pepper slices with the garlic, cilantro, and scallions in the dressing and serve.

SERVES 10

A Valentine's Day Dish

Grilled Breast of Pheasant with Pommes d'Amour and Saffron Risotto

CHEF JONATHAN ZEARFOSS: This dish is truly a personal favorite of mine. I prepared it the night I proposed to my wife Pam. The recipe is full of exciting flavors and sensuous textures while maintaining good nutritional balance. The preparation method is a lean one; grilling does not add any fat, and your guests will be doubly impressed that you are willing to stand outside on a cold winter day to cook the pheasant! If fresh asparagus is available, serve it steamed with this dish.

1 to 1½ cups chicken or vegetable stock (pages 38–39)
Pinch saffron threads
½ teaspoon plus 1 tablespoon extra-virgin olive oil
¼ cup onion, cut into ⅛-inch dice
½ cup arborio rice
6 tablespoons dry white wine
1 tablespoon freshly grated Parmesan cheese
4 pheasant breasts, skinned
2 tablespoons vegetable oil
Kosher salt and freshly ground pepper to taste
2 tomatoes, peeled, seeded, and chopped (see Chef's Tip)

OPTIONAL GARNISH
1 minced fresh or canned black truffle
4 tablespoons unsalted butter at room temperature
Salt and freshly ground pepper to taste

Prepare a grill and preheat the oven to 325°F. Heat ¾ cup of the stock in a small saucepan over low heat and add the saffron. Allow the saffron to steep until the liquid is a deep golden color. Remove from heat.

Heat the ½ teaspoon olive oil in a small sauté pan over medium-low heat and add the onion. Sauté the onion until it is translucent, about 3 minutes, then add the rice and stir until the rice is coated evenly with the oil. Add the saffron-infused stock and wine. Bring the liquid to a simmer, cover, and remove from the heat. Let sit until the rice has absorbed the liquid (about 15 minutes), then spread it in an even layer on a baking sheet. Sprinkle the cheese evenly over the top of the rice. Cover loosely with plastic wrap and refrigerate.

Brush the pheasant breasts lightly with vegetable oil and season with salt and pepper. Over medium coals, grill the pheasant for

(recipe continues)

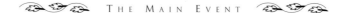

A VALENTINE'S DAY DISH

2½ to 3 minutes on each side. Transfer the pheasant to a baking sheet and place in a 200°F oven while completing the recipe.

Place the partially cooked rice in a shallow saucepan with a little additional stock (just enough to moisten) and simmer 3 to 4 minutes, stirring constantly, until the rice has absorbed all the liquid. It should be hot and have a creamy texture, but still be slightly chewy.

Heat the 1 tablespoon olive oil in a large sauté pan and add the chopped tomatoes. Season with salt and pepper to taste and sauté until hot.

Spoon the saffron risotto along the lower left-hand border of each plate. Spoon the tomatoes in the center alongside the risotto. Top the tomatoes with a pheasant breast.

For a more decadent dish, combine the minced black truffle with butter and salt and pepper, to taste. Top each breast with 1 tablespoon.

SERVES 4

CHEF'S TIP: To prepare peeled, seeded, and chopped tomatoes, begin by removing the core and scoring an x through the skin on the bottom. Submerge into boiling water for 15 seconds. Remove and plunge into ice water. Peel and cut into half around the center or widest part. Squeeze out the seeds and chop.

A CHINESE NEW YEAR FEAST

New Year's Fire Pot ➤ *Steamed Dumplings*

NEW YEAR'S FIRE POT

CHEF SHIRLEY CHENG: This holiday dish is especially suited for gatherings of family and friends. The preparation before the party is simple, and no one person gets stuck in the kitchen doing all of the work. The guests actually cook their own food and eat throughout the evening, as opposed to the Western custom of everyone sitting down at one time and eating a large meal.

4 ounces boneless pork loin

4 ounces boneless chicken breast

4 ounces sole fillet

4 ounces small shrimp, peeled, deveined, and butterflied

4 cups vegetable oil

⅓ cup unsalted peanuts

2 ounces cellophane noodles

10 rectangular wonton wrappers, cut into ¼ inch strips

¼ head Napa cabbage, cored

4 cups packed spinach leaves

4 cups packed watercress sprigs

4 ounces shiitake mushrooms, stemmed

FIRE POT SAUCE

2 tablespoons vegetable oil

2 tablespoons minced fresh ginger

1 cup minced green onions

2 tablespoons hot bean paste (see Chef's Tips)

2 tablespoons mashed salted black beans (see Chef's Tips)

1 tablespoon chili powder

2 tablespoons Chinese rice wine or dry sherry

2 tablespoons light soy sauce

3 tablespoons sugar

2 teaspoons salt

1 tablespoon Asian sesame oil

12 cups chicken stock (page 38)

Cut the pork, chicken, and fish as thinly as possible into slices 1½ inches wide and 2½ inches long. Place each on a separate plate, with the shrimp on a fourth plate.

Pour the oil into a large, heavy saucepan, deep-fryer, or wok. Add the peanuts to the cold oil and place over high heat. When the peanuts are lightly brown, remove and cool. Deep-fry cellophane noodles and wonton wrappers separately in 300°F to

(recipe continues)

A CHINESE NEW YEAR FEAST

325°F oil (almost smoking) until they each puff up and become crisp, about 1 minute each; remove with a slotted utensil and drain on paper towels.

Tear the cabbage, spinach, and watercress leaves into 3-inch pieces. Slice the mushrooms.

To make the sauce: Heat the vegetable oil in a small sauté pan or wok over medium heat and add ginger, green onions, hot bean paste, and black beans. Stir-fry for 10 seconds. Add all the remaining ingredients and bring to a boil; set aside.

Place the fire pot (see Chef's Tips) on a platter. Add 1 cup of cold water to the platter. Pour the sauce in the fire pot. Place all the prepared ingredients around the fire pot. When the sauce starts boiling, each person should begin cooking and eating as desired.

SERVES 6

CHEF'S TIPS: Salted black beans and hot bean paste are available in Asian food markets. The hot bean paste comes as a coarse mixture. You may wish to chop it finer so it blends more smoothly into the sauce.

To set up a fire pot, follow the manufacturer's instructions. If you don't have a fire pot, substitute a fondue pot or an electric fryer—something that will keep the sauce on a low simmer so it is hot enough to cook the meats, seafood, and vegetables. Guests should use chopsticks to dip the morsels into the sauce.

STEAMED DUMPLINGS

CHEF SHIRLEY CHENG: In the Chinese culture, the discovery of a hidden treasure, such as the fortune inside a cookie or the filling in these dumplings, is considered good luck. This simple dumpling is quite nutritious, offering a balance of meat, vegetables, and starch. I enjoy serving this dish at the Chinese New Year, as my way of wishing for good health throughout the year.

DOUGH

3 cups all-purpose flour

1½ cups boiling water

FILLING

1 pound ground pork

½ head Napa cabbage, cored and finely chopped

1 tablespoon minced fresh ginger

1 green onion, minced

2 tablespoons light soy sauce

1 teaspoon salt

1 tablespoon sugar

1 tablespoon Chinese rice wine or dry sherry

1 tablespoon Asian sesame oil

1 teaspoon ground white pepper

1 egg

3 to 5 whole Napa cabbage leaves for steaming

DIPPING SAUCE

1 teaspoon minced fresh ginger

2 teaspoons light soy sauce

3 tablespoons rice vinegar

2 teaspoons sugar

1 teaspoon Asian sesame oil

1 tablespoon chicken stock (see page 38)

To make the dough: In a large bowl, combine the flour and boiling water with a wooden spoon. When cool enough to handle, knead on a lightly floured surface until smooth, and form the dough into a cylinder 2 inches in diameter. Cut the cylinder into 1½-inch pieces and flatten each piece with a small rolling pin into a circle 3½ inches in diameter.

A CHINESE NEW YEAR FEAST

To make the filling: In a large bowl, combine all the ingredients and mix well. Place 1 tablespoon filling in the center of each circle of dough. Fold the wrapper over the filling, forming a half circle. Pinch the edges to seal.

Overlap the cabbage leaves to cover a steamer tray and place the dumplings on top. Cover and steam over boiling water for 15 minutes.

Meanwhile, make the dipping sauce: In a small serving bowl, whisk all the ingredients together. Serve the steamed dumplings at once with the dipping sauce.

MAKES 24 TO 30 DUMPLINGS; SERVES 6 TO 8

CHEF'S TIP: If you don't have a Chinese steamer, you can use a metal vegetable steamer in a pot, or improvise by placing a small bowl or teacup upside down in a pot with 1 or 2 inches of water, then place a plate on top of this, leaving enough room around the edges for steam to circulate. The dumplings can then be placed directly on the plate to steam. If using a steamer rack or tray, the cabbage leaves are necessary to keep the dumplings from sticking.

THE GRAND FINALES

The custom of serving a sweet dish at the end of a meal is said to have been popularized by Catherine de Medici, an Italian noblewoman who later became queen of France. There are many accounts of her enthusiasm for ice cream, and it is believed that this concoction, based on the Italian ice, was perfected to please here.

Regardless of its origins, dessert has become a mainstay of American dining habits, and is now regarded as an all-important final demonstration of the cook's prowess. In fact, dessert has almost become a sign of the personal regard the cook has for his or her guests, and many of us search for new and more elegant ways to conclude a meal.

The desserts in this book are wonderful examples of how simple ingredients can be combined to create rich, delicious sensations. Based on seasonal ingredients such as pumpkin and apples, the impressive dishes in this section offer a range of choices for the final touch to a fall or winter meal.

PUMPKIN DUMPLINGS

CHEF KATHERINE SHEPARD: This fun seasonal dessert may be converted to an accompaniment for a main course of pork, turkey, or game. Simply cut the sugar in half and simmer dumplings in a mixture of half cider and half chicken stock. Don't forget to eliminate the ice cream and pumpkin seeds!

One 16-ounce can pumpkin purée
1¼ cups milk
¼ cup sugar
1 teaspoon salt
1 tablespoon pumpkin pie spice
4 cups all-purpose flour
4 teaspoons baking powder
6 cups apple cider
1 pint vanilla or rum raisin ice cream, melted
½ cup unshelled pumpkin seeds, toasted (see Chef's Tip)

In a large bowl, use an electric hand mixer to combine the pumpkin purée with the milk, sugar, salt, and spice until well blended. Stir the flour and baking powder into the mixture with a wooden spoon to form a soft dough that should just hold its shape on the spoon.

Preheat oven to 200°F. In a medium saucepan, heat the cider to a gentle boil. Form the dough into tablespoon-sized nuggets. Drop 6 to 8 dumplings into the simmering cider. Cook the dumplings until they rise to the surface. Remove with a slotted spoon and place on a baking pan and cover with a damp cloth. Place pan in the oven while continuing to cook the remaining dumplings in batches.

Serve the warm dumplings in a pool of melted ice cream and top with the toasted pumpkin seeds.

MAKES 25 TO 30 DUMPLINGS; SERVES 6 TO 8

CHEF'S TIP: To toast pumpkin seeds, spread cleaned and dried seeds on a baking sheet and toast in a preheated 350°F oven for 6 to 8 minutes, or until lightly browned and beginning to release their aroma.

APPLE AND POPPY SEED CAKE SCENTED WITH LEMON

CHEF RON DESANTIS, C.M.C., AND AMY COLEMAN, M.S., R.D.:
This cake is rich in flavor without the fat, thanks to a fruit purée that provides taste, texture, and moistness. The elimination of shortening has obvious advantages for our waistlines, as well as an interesting historical note. Fruit purées were traditionally used in settlers' times because pantries were usually well stocked with them during fall and winter months when butter was hard to come by. Today, this ingredient has been happily resurrected as an effective, tasty way to trim calories and fat.

4½ cups all-purpose flour
2 tablespoons baking powder
4 eggs
1 teaspoon vanilla extract
1 cup applesauce
1 cup sugar
1½ teaspoons grated lemon zest
2 tablespoons poppy seeds

Preheat the oven to 350°F. Spray a 10-inch bundt pan with vegetable oil spray or coat it with butter and flour.

Sift the flour and baking powder together into a large bowl. In a medium bowl, beat the eggs and add all the remaining ingredients. Mix the egg mixture into the flour until well combined.

Pour the batter into the prepared bundt pan and bake for 1 hour, or until a skewer or toothpick inserted into the center of the cake comes out clean. Place on a rack to cool completely before unmolding.

MAKES 1 CAKE; SERVES 12

CHEF'S TIP: This cake can be prepared in muffin tins for individual servings as well. Decrease baking time to 20 to 25 minutes.

GUGELHOPF

CHEF STACY RADIN: This European cake traditionally contains raisins and almonds, and may have been created to commemorate the defeat of the Turkish army in Vienna in the seventeenth century. The mold is said to look like a Turkish turban. A regular bundt pan can be substituted if you don't have a gugelhopf mold.

½ cup dark raisins
½ cup golden raisins
½ cup dried cherries
Dark rum for soaking
2 cups bread flour
2 cups cake flour
½ tablespoon baking powder
Pinch salt
1 cup (2 sticks) unsalted butter at room temperature
¾ cup granulated sugar
5 eggs
1 cup milk
Grated zest of ½ lemon
Sliced almonds for lining molds
Powdered sugar for dusting

In a small bowl, soak the raisins and dried cherries in dark rum to cover for at least 1 hour. Sift together the bread flour, cake flour, baking powder, and salt. Preheat the oven to 350°F.

In a large bowl, use a hand mixer or an electric mixer with paddle attachment to cream the butter and granulated sugar until light. (Do not whip.) Slowly cream in the eggs, one at a time. Alternately add the milk and sifted dry ingredients in thirds. Drain the dried fruit and add along with the lemon zest.

Grease a 10-inch gugelhopf mold with butter and sprinkle it with sliced almonds. Pour in the batter and bake for about 50 minutes, or until a knife or wooden skewer inserted in the middle comes out clean. Allow the cake to cool in the pan before turning out. Using a fine sieve or sifter, dust with powdered sugar and slice the cake into 16 portions.

MAKES 1 CAKE; SERVES 16

Chocolate Cheesecake with Poached Figs and Passion Fruit and Cherry Sauces

Chef Jonathan Zearfoss: I always served this at the CIA's St. Andrew's Cafe for Valentine's Day. It is especially beautiful when plated using squeeze bottles to paint the two sauces on a dessert plate in the abstract expressionist style of Jackson Pollock.

CRUST

¾ cup hazelnuts

14 graham cracker squares, processed to crumbs

¾ cup fresh orange juice

FILLING

2 cups low-fat cottage cheese

1 cup part-skim ricotta cheese

2 vanilla beans, or 2 teaspoons vanilla extract

4 ounces cream cheese at room temperature

¾ cup honey

2 eggs

1 egg white

3 tablespoons plain nonfat yogurt, drained (see Chef's Tips)

¼ cup cornstarch

½ cup plus 2 tablespoons unsweetened cocoa powder

Poached Figs (recipe follows)

Honey vanilla ice cream (optional)

PASSION FRUIT SAUCE

½ cup passion fruit purée (see Chef's Tips)

¼ cup fresh orange juice

¼ cup fresh grapefruit juice

3 level teaspoons cornstarch

CHERRY SAUCE

¾ cup dried cherries

6 tablespoons sugar

½ cup dry red wine

Small pinch ground cinnamon

2 teaspoons kirsch

Preheat the oven to 300°F. To prepare the crust: Chop the nuts finely in a food processor. Combine in a bowl with the graham cracker crumbs and just enough orange juice to bring the mixture together. Press a thin layer of crust into the bottom of a 9-inch square or 10-inch round baking pan. Bake the crust until it is crisp and resembles a cookie, about 15 minutes.

To prepare the filling: Purée the cottage cheese and ricotta cheese in a food processor. Split the vanilla beans, if using, in half lengthwise and scrape out the pulp. Add the vanilla pulp or the vanilla extract, if using, and all remaining ingredients to the purée and process until smooth. Pour onto the crust.

Place the cake on the middle rack of the oven, then turn the temperature down to 200°F. Place a small bowl of water on the bottom rack of the oven. Bake for 90 minutes or until just set. Remove from the oven and allow to cool to room temperature, then cover and refrigerate.

(recipe continues)

Meanwhile, make the two sauces. To make the passion fruit sauce: Combine the passion fruit purée and juices in a small saucepan. Place several tablespoons of the mixture in a bowl and mix with the cornstarch. Heat the mixture in the pan over medium heat until bubbles begin to appear, then stir and mix in the cornstarch mixture. Bring to a boil. As soon as the sauce thickens, remove immediately and let cool. Transfer to a squeeze bottle or a cup with a spout.

To make the cherry sauce: Place all the ingredients in a small saucepan and add water to cover. Simmer until the cherries are tender, then purée in a blender until smooth. Strain by pressing forcefully through a fine-meshed sieve and let cool. Transfer to a squeeze bottle or a cup with a spout.

When the cheesecake is fully chilled, cut out hearts from the cake with a heart-shaped cookie cutter, or make a paper template and cut around it with a sharp knife. Cover the hearts and refrigerate until ready to serve. Decorate each serving plate, using the two sauces, with a free-form design of drips and splats (see the introductory note). Place a cheesecake heart in the center and a fig half on the side. If you like, add a small scoop of ice cream; serve at once.

SERVES 4 TO 6

CHEF'S TIPS: To drain yogurt, place it in a cheesecloth-lined colander or a fine-meshed sieve over a bowl for 24 hours in the refrigerator.

Passion fruit purée, as well as the purée of other exotic fruits, is becoming increasingly available in specialty food stores. To make it yourself, cut open a passion fruit and scoop out the pulp. Press through a sieve to remove the seeds.

POACHED FIGS

4 teaspoons honey
1 tablespoon sugar
1 tablespoon fresh lemon juice
¼ cup water
4 dried figs

Bring the honey, sugar, lemon juice, and water to boil in a small saucepan. Reduce the heat to a simmer and poach the figs in the syrup until they are cooked but still firm, about 20 to 30 minutes. Split the figs in half and serve warm.

SERVES 4

CHEF'S TIP: The figs can be poached in a microwave on medium heat for 10 minutes.

SOUFFLÉ GLACÉ GRAND MARNIER

CHEF STACY RADIN: This frozen "soufflé" looks just like a hot one, rising several inches above the edge of the ramekin. It also uses the same flavors as a classic soufflé, and is delicate, light and refreshing; however, absolutely no baking is required.

2 cups heavy cream
8 egg yolks
¾ cup granulated sugar
6 tablespoons water
5 tablespoons plus 8 teaspoons Grand Marnier
Grated zest of 1 orange
Unsweetened cocoa powder for dusting
Powdered sugar for dusting

In a deep bowl whip the cream to soft peaks and set aside in the refrigerator. Prepare eight 4-ounce ramekins by wrapping each with a parchment paper collar (see Chef's Tip) extending 1 inch above the rim. Place the ramekins on a baking sheet.

In a large bowl, use an electric mixer to slowly whip the egg yolks until thick. Combine the sugar and water in a small saucepan and bring to a full boil. Gradually add the sugar syrup into the yolks with the mixer on low and continue whipping on high speed until the mixture reaches room temperature. Blend in the 5 tablespoons Grand Marnier and the orange zest.

Gently fold the whipped cream into the mixture by hand. Using a ladle or large spoon, fill each ramekin to ½ inch above rim of ramekin. Flatten the top of the mixture and freeze for 3 to 4 hours.

To serve, unwrap the collars from the ramekins. Pierce 2 holes into each soufflé and pour in 1 teaspoon of the remaining 8 teaspoons Grand Marnier. Using a fine sieve or sifter, dust with cocoa powder and powdered sugar.

SERVES 8

CHEF'S TIP: To prepare the collars, cut 8 strips of parchment paper 1 inch higher and 1 inch longer than the circumference of the ramekins. Rub 1 inch of only one end of the parchment strips with butter. Beginning with the unbuttered end, wrap the parchment around the outside of each ramekin and seal it where it overlaps with the buttered end.

WARM CHOCOLATE SOUFFLÉ PUDDING WITH MILK CHOCOLATE SAUCE

CHEF STACY RADIN: This classic recipe from Austria, where warm desserts are traditional, is a steamed pudding completely unlike the American version of chocolate pudding. A light, airy sensation, it provides a different taste experience.

3 tablespoons butter, melted, plus ¾ cup (1½ sticks) unsalted butter, at room temperature
Powdered sugar for dusting, plus ⅔ cup powdered sugar, sifted
6 egg yolks
3 slices white bread, crusts removed
¼ cup milk
4 squares (4 ounces) semisweet chocolate, chopped
¾ cup fresh bread crumbs
1 cup hazelnuts, toasted and finely ground (see Chef's Tip)
1 tablespoon vanilla extract
10 egg whites
½ cup granulated sugar
Milk Chocolate Sauce (recipe follows)

Brush twelve 6-ounce custard cups with the melted butter. Using a fine sieve or sifter, dust with powdered sugar and shake out the excess. Place the cups in a baking pan with 2-inch sides. Preheat the oven to 350°F.

In a large bowl, use a hand mixer or electric mixer with paddle attachment to cream the ¾ cup butter and the ⅔ cup powdered sugar until light and smooth. Slowly cream in the egg yolks one at a time.

In a shallow bowl, soak the bread in the milk. Melt the chocolate over simmering water, stirring until smooth. Mix melted chocolate into the butter mixture. Add the soaked bread, bread crumbs, nuts, and vanilla and blend.

In a large bowl, combine the egg whites and granulated sugar and whip until medium-stiff peaks of meringue are formed. Fold into the chocolate base.

Fill the prepared cups three fourths full. Add warm water to the baking pan to reach halfway up sides of cups and bake until set, about 40 minutes. Remove from the oven and take cups from

(recipe continues)

the water bath and allow to cool down. While the soufflé is still warm, turn the cups upside down and unmold onto a dessert plate. If the soufflé sticks to the cups, gently free up around the edges with a paring knife. Serve warm with milk chocolate sauce.

SERVES 12

CHEF'S TIP: To prepare the hazelnuts for the soufflé pudding, spread out coarsely ground nuts on a baking sheet and toast in a preheated 350°F oven for about 10 minutes, or until lightly golden brown. Toss frequently in order to brown evenly. After toasting, grind the nuts again in a food processor to achieve an even finer texture. Either skinned or unskinned hazelnuts may be used.

MILK CHOCOLATE SAUCE

1 cup heavy cream
2 tablespoons honey
1 heaping cup (7 ounces) milk chocolate, finely chopped
Vanilla extract to taste

Combine the cream and honey in a small saucepan over medium heat and bring to a boil. Remove from the heat and add the chocolate and vanilla. Stir until the chocolate is completely melted. Serve warm.

MAKES ABOUT 2 CUPS

White Chocolate Almond Crème Brûlée

CHEF STACY RADIN: The direct translation of *crème brûlée* is "burnt cream," and that is a fairly accurate description! Crème brûlée is enjoying new popularity in America. The classic version is vanilla, but variations are being created across the country. Rich and succulent, crisp and creamy, hot and cold, the contrasts in flavor, texture, and temperature make it a luscious ending to a fine meal.

2 cups heavy cream
½ cup, plus 8 teaspoons sugar
½ vanilla bean, split lengthwise
3 squares (3 ounces) white chocolate, finely chopped
   (see Chef's Tips)
5 egg yolks
3 tablespoons Amaretto

Place eight 4-ounce ramekins in a baking pan with 2-inch sides. Preheat the oven to 325°F.

In a medium saucepan, combine the heavy cream, the ½ cup sugar, and vanilla bean over medium-high heat and bring to a boil. Remove from the heat and add the chocolate, stirring until melted.

In a medium bowl, whisk the egg yolks until light and frothy. Gradually mix in about ½ cup of the boiled cream mixture, stirring constantly. Slowly pour the yolk mixture back into the remaining cream mixture, stirring constantly. Strain the custard through a fine-meshed sieve. Stir in the liqueur. Pour the custard into the ramekins.

Fill the baking pan with warm water halfway up the sides of the ramekins and bake for 30 to 40 minutes, or until set. Remove from the oven and allow to cool. Cover with plastic wrap and refrigerate until ready to serve.

To serve, preheat the broiler. Sprinkle the surface of each custard with 1 teaspoon sugar. Place the ramekins under the broiler about a minute until sugar melts and caramelizes; take care not to burn (see Chef's Tips).

SERVES 8

VARIATION: Cover the surface of the custards with toasted slivered almonds (page 90) and sprinkle with powdered sugar. Brown as instructed.

CHEF'S TIPS: White chocolate may be purchased at gourmet stores or confectionary shops.

Be careful when melting the sugar under the broiler. If left too long under the broiler, the sugar will burn and the custard will become too soft.

APPLE STRUDEL

CHEF MARKUS FARBINGER, C.M.P.C. (EUROPEAN): This is a classic Austrian dish, and one that has been passed down from generation to generation in my family. Many people consider strudel dough difficult to make; however, my grandmother and my mother taught me, and I know you can learn it too. Don't be afraid to handle the dough, because pulling and stretching it is necessary! This a wonderful recipe for fall, when apples are at their best.

DOUGH
4 cups sifted bread flour
1 teaspoon salt
3 tablespoons vegetable oil, plus more for coating
1 cup plus 2 tablespoons water

FILLING
¾ cup dried cranberries
¼ cup dark rum
¾ cup granulated sugar
1 teaspoon ground cinnamon
4 tablespoons (½ stick) unsalted butter, plus ¾ cup (1½ sticks)
   unsalted butter, melted
½ cup dried fresh bread crumbs
5 pounds (about 12) cooking apples (such as Mutsu, Ida Red, or
   Granny Smith), cored, quartered, and thinly sliced, skin left on
¼ cup fresh lemon juice
Powdered sugar, for dusting

To make the dough: Using an electric mixer with a dough hook or a food processor with the dough blade, combine the flour, salt, 3 tablespoons oil, and water and mix on high speed until smooth and elastic, 10 to 12 minutes. Shape the dough into a fairly smooth ball and coat with a small amount of oil. Cover with plastic wrap and let the dough rest for 1 hour at room temperature or overnight in the refrigerator.

To make the filling: Soak the cranberries in the rum in a small bowl. In another bowl, combine the granulated sugar and cinnamon. In a medium sauté pan over medium heat, melt 4 tablespoons butter and sauté the bread crumbs until golden brown, about 5 minutes. Set aside. In a large bowl, toss together the apples, cranberries, cinnamon-sugar mixture, and lemon juice. Set aside. Preheat the oven to 375°F.

Using an entire table surface, about 4 feet long, lay a clean tablecloth or sheet over the surface and sprinkle the cloth with flour. Roll the strudel dough as thinly as possible with a rolling pin in all directions. (Remove any jewelry and watch at this point.) Working carefully, place your hands under the dough with your palms down and use the back of your hands to stretch the dough very thin until it is translucent. Work all of the dough until it is a fairly even thinness and forms a rectangle.

Brush some of the melted butter over the surface of the dough. Spread the sautéed bread crumbs over the lower third of the dough. Spread the apple mixture over the bread crumbs. Trim away about one quarter inch of the dough's perimeter: the area that is thicker and not evenly flat. Beginning at the edge covered in apples, begin rolling up the strudel, jelly-roll style. Use the tablecloth to help you roll by gripping it and lifting it gently forward. Pinch both ends of the rolled strudel to seal. Place the strudel, seam-side down, on a baking sheet covered with parchment or waxed paper (curve the strudel to form an S to fit the pan). Brush the strudel with the remaining melted butter. Bake until golden and tender when pierced with a knife, about 30 minutes.

Remove from the oven and, using a fine sieve or sifter, dust with powdered sugar. Cut immediately into 2-inch slices and serve warm.

MAKES 2 DOZEN 2-INCH PORTIONS

CHEF'S TIP: The strudel dough may also be made by hand. Mound the flour onto a clean work surface. Create a well in the center and add the salt, oil, and water. Incorporate the flour into the liquid a little at a time by working your fingertips in a circular motion from the center of the well outward. Once the dough has come together and all the flour has been combined, begin kneading by hand. After about 10 minutes the dough should be smooth and elastic. Shape into a ball and proceed as described above.

CHUNKY APPLE GRANITÉ WITH APPLE CRISPS

CHEF MARKUS FÄRBINGER, C.M.P.C. (EUROPEAN): This is a very refreshing dessert on a hot summer's day. A granité is a coarser and crunchier alternative to sorbet. However, if you have an ice cream freezer available, you can make sorbet with this recipe by freezing the mixture according to the manufacturer's instructions.

1½ cups sugar
1 cup water
4 teaspoons clover honey or pure maple syrup
¾ cup fresh lemon juice
2 Granny Smith apples, cored and cut into ¼-inch dice, skin left on
5 Granny Smith apples, cored and puréed, skin left on
Apple Crisps (recipe follows)

Place a baking pan or cake pan for the granité into the freezer to prechill.

Place sugar, water, honey or maple syrup, and 2 tablespoons of lemon juice in a small saucepan. Bring to a boil and lower heat to below a simmer. Add diced apples and poach until translucent, about 5 minutes. Strain, cover, and refrigerate the apples. Reserve the syrup.

In a food processor, purée the cored whole apples, remaining lemon juice, and reserved syrup. Pour the purée into the prechilled pan and return to the freezer. Stir with a whisk every 2 hours. After 6 hours, the granité should become dry and granular. Mix in the refrigerated diced apples. Spoon into dishes and serve with Apple Crisps on the side.

MAKES 2 QUARTS

APPLE CRISPS

2 Granny Smith apples, cored, skin left on
½ cup sugar
1 tablespoon butter

Preheat the oven to 300°F. Using the fine blade of a food processor, or by hand, slice apples as thinly as possible crosswise into circles. Sprinkle one side of each slice lightly with sugar. Place, sugared-side down, on a baking sheet covered with buttered parchment or waxed paper. Bake until golden brown, about 12 minutes. Let cool to room temperature.

MAKES ABOUT 2 DOZEN CRISPS

VARIATION: Instead of granulated sugar, sprinkle the apples with brown sugar, cinnamon sugar, or vanilla sugar.

CHEF'S TIP: Apple crisps may also be eaten by themselves as a low-fat snack. Stored in an airtight container in a cool, dry place; they will keep for up to 1 week. Do not refrigerate, as they will become soft and sticky.

INDEX

TABLE OF EQUIVALENTS

The exact equivalents in the following tables have been rounded for convenience.

US/UK

US/UK	METRIC
oz=ounce	g=gram
lb=pound	kg=kilogram
in=inch	mm=millimeter
ft=foot	cm=centimeter
tbl=tablespoon	ml=milliliter
fl oz=fluid ounce	l=liter
qt=quart	

WEIGHTS

US/UK	METRIC
1 oz	30 g
2 oz	60 g
3 oz	90 g
4 oz (¼ lb)	125 g
5 oz (⅓ lb)	155 g
6 oz	185 g
7 oz	220 g
8 oz (½ lb)	250 g
10 oz	315 g
12 oz (¾ lb)	375 g
14 oz	440 g
16 oz (1 lb)	500 g
1½ lb	750 g
2 lb	1 kg
3 lb	1.5 kg

OVEN TEMPERATURES

FAHRENHEIT	CELSIUS	GAS
250	120	½
275	140	1
300	150	2
325	160	3
350	180	4
375	190	5
400	200	6
425	220	7
450	230	8
475	240	9
500	260	10

LIQUIDS

US	METRIC	UK
2 tbl	30 ml	1 fl oz
¼ cup	60 ml	2 fl oz
⅓ cup	80 ml	3 fl oz
½ cup	125 ml	4 fl oz
⅔ cup	160 ml	5 fl oz
¾ cup	180 ml	6 fl oz
1 cup	250 ml	8 fl oz
1½ cups	375 ml	12 fl oz
2 cups	500 ml	16 fl oz
4 cups/1 qt	1 l	32 fl oz

EQUIVALENTS FOR COMMONLY USED INGREDIENTS

ALL-PURPOSE (PLAIN) FLOUR/ DRIED BREAD CRUMBS/CHOPPED NUTS

¼ cup	1 oz	30 g
⅓ cup	1½ oz	45 g
½ cup	2 oz	60 g
¾ cup	3 oz	90 g
1 cup	4 oz	125 g

WHOLE-WHEAT (WHOLEMEAL) FLOUR

3 tbl	1 oz	30 g
½ cup	2 oz	60 g
⅔ cup	3 oz	90 g
1 cup	4 oz	125 g
1¼ cups	5 oz	155 g
1⅔ cups	7 oz	210 g
1¾ cups	8 oz	250 g

BROWN SUGAR

¼ cup	1½ oz	45 g
½ cup	3 oz	90 g
¾ cup	4 oz	125 g
1 cup	5½ oz	170 g
1½ cups	8 oz	250 g

WHITE SUGAR

¼ cup	2 oz	60 g
⅓ cup	3 oz	90 g
½ cup	4 oz	25 g
¾ cup	6 oz	185 g
1 cup	8 oz	250 g
1½ cups	12 oz	375 g

RAISINS/CURRANTS/SEMOLINA

¼ cup	1 oz	30 g
⅓ cup	2 oz	60 g
½ cup	3 oz	90 g
¾ cup	4 oz	125 g
1 cup	5 oz	155 g

LONG-GRAIN RICE/CORNMEAL

⅓ cup	2 oz	60 g
½ cup	2½ oz	75 g
¾ cup	4 oz	125 g
1 cup	5 oz	155 g
1½ cups	8 oz	250 g

DRIED BEANS

¼ cup	1½ oz	45 g
⅓ cup	2 oz	60 g
½ cup	3 oz	90 g
¾ cup	5 oz	155 g
1 cup	6 oz	185 g
1¼ cups	8 oz	250 g
1½ cups	12 oz	375 g

ROLLED OATS

⅓ cup	1 oz	30 g
⅔ cup	2 oz	60 g
1 cup	3 oz	90 g
1½ cups	4 oz	125 g
2 cups	5 oz	155 g